**Marginal
Future**

By the same author

The Long Interval/Four from Northern Women (Bloodaxe, 1986)
Half Light (Camberwell School of Art 1988) with Rachel Levitas
Flowers of Fever (Iron Press, 1992)
The Apple Exchange (Flambard, 1999)
The Work of the Wind (Flambard, 2006)
The Homage (Iron Press, 2006)
The Absolute Bonus of Rain (Flambard, 2010)
Composition in White (Smokestack, 2017)

Edited
Light from a Black Hole (Waddington Street Centre, 1997)
Free to Fly (Teesdale Community Health Services Centre, 1998)
The Poetry of Perestroika (Iron Press, 1991)

Selected Anthologies
Seven Years On (Green Book Press, 1986)
Modern Poets of Northern England (Raduga Press,1988)
New Women Poets (Bloodaxe, 1990)
Forward Book of Poetry 2001
North by North-East (Iron Press, 2006)
Both Sides of Hadrian's Wall (Lapwing Press, 2006)
Not Just a Game (Five Leaves, 2006)
Wilds (Ek Zuban, 2007)
Poetry etc (Masthead Literary Arts, 2009)
Land of Three Rivers (Bloodaxe, 2017)
The Brown Envelope Book (Caparison, 2021)
Bread and Roses Poetry Anthology 2021 (Culture Matters, 2021)

Marginal
Future
SJ Litherland

Smoke
STACK
BOOKS

Smokestack Books
School Farm
Nether Silton
Thirsk
North Yorkshire
YO7 2JZ
e-mail: info@smokestack-books.co.uk
www.smokestack-books.co.uk

ISBN 9781739473471
Smokestack Books
is represented by
Inpress Ltd

*for Nye, Sam, Arthur,
Joe, my four grandsons*

'Close the Coalhouse Door,
lads, there's blood inside.'
Alex Glasgow

'You're either a Taker or a Giver.'
Auntie Janet

'human kind
Cannot bear
very much reality.'
TS Eliot

Contents

My Mother's House

The Valley

Guest List in January

I have set my table with six place mats.
My mother's glass table, newly arrived,
is ready for non guests. The woven mats
are moon rings of black and dried grass,
earthy and elegant. No one sits with me.

Who are my uninvited guests enlivening
my January days, days of shallows
and deep shadows, the crossing of a bird,
solitary, in my yard? The wire brushes
of trees, slanted wet roofs windowed?

Derek Walcott is one and Ian Bell, artists
of beauty and form like constant seascapes
of ribbonned waves arriving without pause.
Whitby is another, the town and harbour,
its khaki beaches under wild nets of sea haze.

The sea's unsatisfied appetite is welcome
at my table. Next to Whitby will sit falling snow,
the first of winter's sacrifices from dark skies.
By its side snowdrops from a moortop grave.
When guests are gone, the dead will visit.

Tiredness Now is Frailty

Unsteadiness on a wave of displacement
comes in a movement you steer through
but the sensation is frequent, the ground
temporal and you are walking on air,
a vanishing but you are still here, a ghost
in your own life staggering around your home.

You want to doctor it with vitamins, fruit,
and the blood tonic of garlic, a poultice
of remedies, and the wisp of dizziness
is a wasp, the scout of an army, buzzing.
Tiredness comes in a shroud, there's less
and there will be less recovery, despite

the walking in the Vale which is the journey
of the frail heart which strengthens,
you emerge from the hawthorn sprays,
the bluebells and pink bells, the holly trees
with their verdant soft prickles, soft as skin
of a baby, your legs *pistoned*, head clear,

into another late mist, a bank of giddiness
you walk through as atoms flow past
dissolving, a sea without purchase, like the days
when a name juggles in your mind. What stays
is arguing on waking, as if the world listens,
words still working in the mills of logic.

A Sense of Bereavement

November 2015: for Ian Bell, dropped from the England team

He lit up my life: my sorrow that of age
with winter starting. Winter's frozen
tears on the pavement, harbinger
of silent depression on my own, ringed

by Sunday newspapers: the griefs of Paris
are deadly separation of lover and lover,
the young in constant occupation
of war's battlefield. And here's a lesser

grief if we must measure. What I
remember, just a scrap, was the egret
taking off, melody of wings and grass
and in the poetry and the presence, pages
of white paper fluttering like notes.

He was that figure, the artist kneeling
in joy and ecstasy as he performed
a miracle of gesture and hit the ball
with the unfolding of the bird's wings.

Today the months are empty, no time
put aside to watch something exquisite
in the service of a game. We're left
with something less than marvellous.

About Women

I Death of a Marriage

after The Bowl of Milk (Pierre Bonnard)

The cat calls me to duty mewing from the floor.

I move in an altered landscape, a lost territory.
Her insistence she is half fed and half starved.

Every material thing is still in place but my heart.
A jug of milk on the desk, the peonies in the vase.

The river has highlights but the shade is dark.
Stopped in a frame I move with time stationary.

All before this moment is past, all after terror.
Motionless with the bowl of milk in my hand

I cannot see the end of day or the end of night.
I am unable to leave this interrupted scene

or walk out of the room. For the rest of my life
I am a woman in a coral gown with red hair.

The shadow on the desk will never move across.
The peonies never droop. The cat never

receive her milk. This is the death of happiness.

II *Incompleteness*

What her heart tells her would be incompleteness.
A small trouble will not loom larger.
What her heart holds will not be empty.

If she were a fabric she would be crumpled.
Her heart tells her a meal partaken of
will be her scent, her favourite perfume.
The weather by the sea will be changeable.

Her heart tells her she is anguished.
The weather by the sea will not be changeable.
An injury will not be deadly.

Her heart tells her a sudden thought
is not a warning.
The cherry blossom is a bird.
A sparrow is a flower.

A part of her body is broken.
Her heart tells her she is not
an occasional song, nor a part thereof.

If she were an unknowing it would be
incompleteness.

III *Madame Swann*

after the painting by Rachel Levitas

She with her blue mood
    and still young breasts
her hair ballooning
    into a neat headdress

 one hand tentative
    almost protective.

Dismissed
    from diaries of his life
on a nod complicit
    with falling flowers.

She is scored into fabric
    with a pencil of light

all that remains of desire
    all that remains of fire
is the outline we draw
    around dead feeling.

    I did not see the tear
the single tear from
    her frozen eyes.

The mouth not firm
    but like a bird flying
about to leave her face
    tilted for the blow.

IV *Tisane*

The discounted woman
has nothing to say.

Today I dress in yellow
with embroidered birds

in artifice of yesterday.
Lay a tray with a teacup

on linen. At the top
of the garden at four

in the ceremony
of drinking tisane

I put my despair in a box
and tie it with ribbon.

Each scissor sharp pain
folded away in tissue.

Traces of how I stood vacantly
cannot be revoked.

V The Mind Moth

The mind opens and the word *Vapourer* flies in
    a lowly moth a moth of no colour a mind moth

a grey room where a psychiatrist lay on a couch
    and told stories to the ceiling in cigarette smoke

a shy woman on a new estate
    built up to the thin fence of the main road

a boat that refuses to turn around
    hypnotised by the swell of the sea

    so like low murmurs of death
indistinguishable in the night
    when we do not wake

caught in a net
    a time traveller who came to our shores
and lived in the bottom of dark vales

flew into a pattern on muslin
    copied from cave walls
like a wayward doodle

like a wayward boat
    stubborn in its directionless future

the Vapourer has melted into pure
    vodka   a killer cocktail with a single black olive
    like a floating bomb

the mind closes forever

drinking the looking glass water

the *Vapourer* is the final dark smudge on her lips.

Femme

A breeze of scent; I kissed her goodbye at the train,
my daughter and her tall son, the perfume in the rain,

just drops, the air fragrant, just April, the Northern trees
in bud and nothing to look forward to, the train agrees

with its sharp whistles. *I like your perfume* I said at once.
She smiled. *It's yours.* It ought to have signalled France

and end-of-the-line *Femme*; it was my mother's scent
which became discontinued. *Oh, no, too astringent!*

We are in a tiny shop in East Dulwich, a woman fixes
a sample. *As near as you can to Femme*? Offers three mixes

on a stick. Scents compete like wallflowers at a dance.
I take away in a bottle the concocted chance

to summon the three of us with identical perfume,
blossoming at that moment of singular time

in the days of long dresses and ropes of beads, scent
we never expected to fade or vanish, still present.

The Move

The back yard – I deserted it – the colliery slabs laid
down in 1860
more decent than mud. I walk there over the moss and
dark edges.
Turn at the bent latch of the gate. Time holds the past
in cheerful
bright prints – no sepia – and my feet halt as I look down.
Not a dream –
handcuffed to the physical textual loss. Cross the
threshold
there is my back room, the fireplace of many irons,
large Durham pots,
the black range, rescued from its own history –
I walk
up the stairs between the crossed arms of the black
banister
and silver dado. I stay on the landing. It's the last visit. I do
not enter
my bedrooms, nor my front room. It's not a lonely vigil.
It's life.

Studentland

Tell them   the way noises of backyards
are fires you cannot put out   the noises
of bombardments   shrapnel   sharp loud voices

scratching the night.   You don't know where fires
will light up   the heavy black sounds   exploding.

You end up where you began
in a shelter where you can't sleep   war thuds

electric pathways   students coming home 3 am
a barbed wire trail of screams.

Silence has never felt so distant

the preservation of night   in the war the night
was full of alarms.   Patrols of students

in drunken lurches up the street
                    it hits you in the midriff of sleep.

And jubilation
will descend in the midnight hours
thud thud thud
                    of drums
                              like Ack Ack guns.

You sit in tense attitudes
as if waiting for the blow. You pick up the phone.

You wait for sudden quiet
like the sound of the *All Clear*.

                    Your heart over-beats   listens in a shell.

Insistent repetitive music   the whoops   tribal ribald chants

as if they need to bellow
as if they are beasts rounded up by prods of doubt and alcohol.

Paths sweat with leaves
                    and empty packets of this and that.

Don't cry
for these homes and backyards
                            the lawn you kept mowing
in the wilderness   they're already dead
                                    with no heartbeat or breath.

Fox Country

after a painting by Rachel Levitas

Under the sun and summer of flowers
our shadowed country, our darker lives,

predators in the open, foxes and flowers fight
for space, harmony an illusion,

and the sensation of light is the world
constantly turning from its own shadow.

The universe busy exchanging atoms,
the flux of particles in deep time, the fox,

like us, alive for a moment, survival
prompts him. The age blooms yellow

and rose. The flag of our country is dark
and dirty, rained on, left on the table

of the century. Fox grasps what's to come,
caught in the act, warns us, knows us.

Counter Culture

A derelict car park café for top scenes
over London, insouciance ahead
of the trend and billionaire lock-ins,

you can breathe the air of old markets;
the futures are not for sale; unmanned
galleries and eternal avant-garde
stapled on walls; artists have moved south
like terns, flocks appoint what's depleted
into hideaways for the cognoscenti,

Peckham the cultural landscape
we're always seeking beneath the capital
trademarks, where poets and painters shift

their wares, Bohemia that comes and goes
like the tidal river that snakes through City banks:
the collectives, the communes, the free spirit
and in tall towers, spikes, and otherwise columns
of money, they're unaware and too square.
Irritating what money can't buy in their highrise

systems, dry with air conditioning and precise
desk tops, the huge stairways in their atriums.
It's money talking suits, striped shirts and gyms.

Infiltration has begun in Catford and Eltham,
old gangland corners of South London,
moving waves that defeat the consortium:
below their eyes, their charts, their self-esteem;
artists pay no attention to austerity
and bad vibes. They're not bought or sold.

They don't recognise that currency.

Last Rites

for Max Levitas

What he practises is to get out of bed
for visitors, daughters of his brother.
He is about to die while sleeping in calm
possession of death. He must listen
to another visitor, son of his brother,
he must listen to the story of the march,
the drums of the world are drumming.
It is not a good sign. His eagle eyes
are curious. He has stopping eating
but this is food, the food of talk.
He is a man about to die while sleeping,
wrapped in the shawl of death.
He was part of that movement,
that lifted itself, rearing like judgement.

Marginal
Future

Marginal Future

I leave behind the viaduct and train cars like shooting stars.
Our love lines were girded by railway and pastoral back yards.

The little light on the wardrobe – itself a relic from the past –
a boat light – is unlit. You're not here yet. I leave you to ghost
the house deep in the valley with familiar rooms in my head:

the yellow room, the silver wainscot on the stairs, the bedroom
painted red, the rose leaf fall of the cherry tree now dead, poems
of conjugal rites and lapses of conviction, I leave you

in the house always in the past tense. I move out to
a marginal future, the sea of years is scuttled of water,
the beautiful horizon a parade of trees like green waves

but the years creep to shallows. It is fitting I live on a hill
and greet the weather to come, the sunset in long ribbons,
County Hall has fading firelight on its roof. The verse

moves on, words will not be dumb, words tattoo flesh
and walls, words choose a chisel, the new house is stencilled.

The Risen Wood

i
Shock of the white woods
white as cold china, ethereal
and fragile in their finery,

as if winter was widowhood
eternal and compulsory.

ii
Winter trees in the Vale
demure in pink veils
none as fine as the white
limbed slender birches

> *like girls in the Fifties*
> *with half hats perched*
> *cloudy with net haloes*

their smoky pink so sheer
dark branches behind
etch through outlines.

> *Trees blush like a maiden.*

iii
Behold the risen wood

a curtain lifting on spring
stitches of lime and pink

trees fanning out
lift delicate mosaic
towards the equinox

> so close to sacred.

Unsettlement

Trees are now in leaf even the laggard.
The house and I sit together. A stranger,
foreign stairs and balustrade. I sit alone

on the balcony. I had to breach the door
against deep waves pressing me not to enter,
this new place with its crows-nest view.

I abandoned my home in the valley.
No-one to mend the gate and fallen wall.
It's my past which makes it beautiful.

The world is a tapestry carefully stitched.
If only my mind would not sit like this.
The dandelions have seized the lawn

with brazen lamps. The garden is falling
into seed. I understand the notes of work
the birds sing, always calling when we rest.

The health of a house is visible.
The peace of the newly polished,
the washed clothes, the tidy-up.

The deep waves are holding me down
like gravity, I sit in my new glass house,
nothing out there but unreality.

The Moment as Memoir

The day has just slipped by
the best of it reading Nabokov,
snob, raconteur, the maker

of phrases that flow like a river.

He is not sensitive, unlike Proust,
his hive alive with a thousand bees
serving himself the carried honey,

his memoir glides into shadows.

I sit on the balcony and read,
claiming the sun in stripes across
rigid paving. The trees no longer bright.

The trees in shade a forest green.

Dark folds hold the end of August.
Dark jade massed below like a reef.

The last of sunshine catches the ridge
like a wave cresting on the foliage.

No time for memoir, the ebb is one way.
Their shadow enters my reading.
The past is the moment the light dies.

Early Morning Moment

A string of white birds flew
sunlit like a bar of music across

the dark green Vale, and another
entered, drawn into the reprise,

white birds pegged on a moving line.
They were gone, the valley silent.

The trees still written upon.

Circlet

In Flass the way the light plays
there is a tree suddenly white
as if the shock of the news
of Erica, the sudden soon
loss of her without warning,
the week long, that is all,
the week of her life-blood
ebbing like the wilt of pansies
in a moment, cast down
from their faces upturned
to stalks lying flat and yellow.

In Flass the way the light plays
amongst the green a tree whitens
as if for Erica and her cheerfulness,
the shock of the news like wind
on the leaves, and on pansies
wilting in their pots overnight,
as if bright faces and upright
limbs are not read by the future
and the strewn down circlet
of fallen stems is like the loss
of Erica, unforeseen.

At the Gates of Winter

Here, birds suddenly ready to leave.

Northern clouds cold as seawater
dim the autumn lights of the trees.

The east wind has sent her warning.
No more hesitation, the long autumn
in gold livery is losing threads in raiment.

A grey mantle driven over the Vale,
the east wind enters the wood slyly
from behind, the Queen of the East
with her grey hood and sharp tongue.

You can stay indoors and weaken.

Her cuts are razor-sharp like a penance.
First frost is laying the lawn to rest.
We're at the gates of the cemetery.

Untitled

Against the trees snow
is undecided: *sleet /*
rain / snow / not cold
enough for a blizzard.

It's February, the birds
are pairing, they love-dive
at wing length. The snow
sharpens in the vice

of winter and yet
snow is epiphany, lace
cascades across the valley,
splinters of the Snow Queen's

heart, her thrall of cruelty,
don't drive in it / don't fall.
Who is sending fits of rain?
The undrawn grey curtains?

Clouds

Dove grey /

sky net of finest pink
delicate mesh

slab grey fingers   dark fish
deep sea fish   sea flora

with wing claws / talons
to scrape a passage

blunt fingers of cloud tide /

scarves and throat wisps

cross-hatching
and rubbings out

and fading light / clarity /

Rothko's pink period /
suicide

sunset
beneath the horizon

Bad News

The years are narrow as gulls feet on sand.
Illness is not a metaphor but a cloud at sea,
stationary, I had thought about that, not
your voice closed with something hard
to say, wayward as a shift of time, like falling
asleep and waking in another room, slow
words fall like grenades mining the future,
betraying us to the spectrum of fear without
warning, no readiness in the leaves, or bones,
no stirring of the senses, no apprehension.
Someone innocent caught in the net.
We share the bond. We would take the burden,
take the pain, take the fear, but the young
hold the threaded needle for the next stitch.

Cloud without Rain

The mood has lifted on drought
as rain sprinkles just enough

on lawns and stifled flowers.
I have lost sheltered ferns.

Single haughty tulips suffer,
withered as crepe paper.

At night like a lamplighter
I replenished the pansies.

The cold dry skies of April
did not release their fists.

Purposeless clouds too thin
to cheer us up. And now rain drips

like the beginning of talk
like any beginning of remote

possibilities, stops too soon,
a small respite, a small oasis

I should be grateful for. This
spring of the cloud without rain.

Drought in the North

Dark clouds break up somehow
and sail over in ragged fleece
over a sea of threatening blue
heat returning through all that promise.

Weary of taps and the hose and sad
patient roses, the stultified lilies,
brown patched skin of lawn,
drought in the throats of plants.

The cricket fields are biscuit dry.

Will rain come tapping on skylights?
Or rattle on my conservatory
in downpour like cicadas at noon
plunging saws into Spanish trees?

We're far from that. The applause
of rain is forgotten by the nation.

Claws of drought are deeper each day.
Winter stores raided for pasture,
sheep lie by walls panting like dogs.
The hay meadows are stillborn.

Outpouring

O lowly rain, the lowest of rain, persistent and mild,
one that is steady but has lulls and throws of little stones
on the conservatory. The clattering of rain horses.
And the Vale trees are whitened across the valley.
I greet you courteously after the heat
rising
day by day
withstood by the flowers ageing before my eyes,
too much sun in their veins. Mist in the trees

    puffs like smoke. It never felt more like a blessing,

dismaying to pleasure of picnics, cricket, days out.
Our patio dreams over-riding the indoor light, dull
and inconvenient, as if every day is a holiday.
The earth welcomes clouds as we welcome the sun
yearning for its treasure. Rain is workmanlike, labouring,
doing its job. The valley teaches another measure.
The rising mist
is steam
vanishing as it cools, like an afterthought,

    like smoke hazarding the trees reprieved by rain.

Apologia

Relief of incessant rain, rain with no morals.
Rain on the parade. Rain that comes in gallons.

Nothing is close to the delight of heavy rain.
The plants are splashed all over. No rules.

Rain that goes to the heart of the garden.

The trills and vibratos, the crescendos.
I thank the rain gods for their pity,
their divine intervention. I cursed them

for looking the other way and driving
their chariots to the edge of the sky

where the rain drifts were clearly visible
as billowing curtains of downpours.
I stayed indoors to reflect on privation.

Unjustly.

Paramin

i.m. Derek Walcott

A greeting to hills and the high village of Paramin
to the poet who bequeathed its secret rhythm.

Morning to Kingston, Antigua, Barbados and Port of Spain
the cities and shores, the forest thickets uncombed.

The seas will break your back on entering unwisely.

Morning to the long beaches the colour of pearl
and the lion that growls in the waves, the ageing poet

with his power undiminished, seeking the morning
with his Judah roar, poetry rushes into the air with birds

inattentive to his final hour. He dies before the morning.

Morning to the cricketers who pack their whites.
And I greet again the match in Sabina Park to watch

the eclipse of the England team and electric storm

of black arms raised to the heavens, to the rain
of wickets and noughts like storm drops on the board.

I miss the language we all share, the poet's tongue.

Unbound

The figure floodlit in the gloom, twilight
cloaks him when only boundaries will do.

He is left to strike tableaux in silhouette
after crossing and recrossing the square,

after patience at the loom; time to set aside
the workmanlike as darkness closes in.

His calligraphic bat has one word to write.

Like an executioner with his blade,
the imprint hangs against the fading light,

The shape held like a statue, the figure
and stroke consensual in the gesture.

Balancing beauty with service, beauty
the higher reach until one run is enough.

The cloak of the night is off his shoulders.

A Page from The Book of Changes

The birds have entered the garden
like words have entered this page
  on stalks of the pen. Four blue tits

peck a stump in Chinese symmetry.

A black cat levers over the fence
sinuous as a cobra. Abruptly I open
a door. I am the guardian.

The garden returns to emptiness.

If I hang food it will magnetise
the garden. I hesitate between
intervention and negligence,

the lawn an oasis of open ground.

The Vale of trees is motherly
to the birds, hill folds wrap them
in leaf cloaks, gold and russet.

opulent like furs in Russia
  becoming frayed at the edges.

The plumage of trees is falling.

They will show stalks. I will wait
for dead winter to feed the birds.
  A moment changes. The cat entered

the poem and scattered words.

Interregnum

The Language of Gesture

for Steve Walker & Peter Mortimer

In Russia there is no misunderstanding. Gestures
are dangerous. Never express approval!
We were at dinner in the flat of the puppet master
who had shown us rooms of his mechanical toys
which should have been a warning of overkill,
they had the air of the mad scientist. Seated
with us at dinner was his favourite puppet,
the lifelike beauty, not mannequin more companion.
Her eyelashes were like a flower arrangement
of ferns. She sat among our conversation.
We moved to leave. He spoke to Steve directly
who had admired her: next to him a full-size doll.
'She loves you!' The puppet master was clear.
She was very sad. 'Take her with you!' He was Svengali
with his puppets, knew her unspoken soul.
The gesture was an iron fist. A gift, he said.
Steve carried her back to our hotel under his arm.
A strange lifeless body. 'I can't take her to my room.'
Russia was this country of impossible demands.
The hotel a gift from Stalin in one of his moods.
It was shaped like a rigid trifle with turrets.
At the entrance chandeliers and a large echoing hall
guarded by a desk and the keeper of keys.
Opposite were ranks of lockers. He stuffed her
in one of these. Her legs stuck out. She was still there
next morning. On the plane he had to have two seats.

They waved goodbye. We never asked what happened next.

1987

48

The Interregnum

in the USSR: November–December 1991; August 1987
for Peter Mortimer

I

Like refugees we padded down the corridor
for early morning tea in Russian winter light

thrice sealed windows   outside snow
and the falling rouble. The huge samovar
of domed silver   the little tap

the scent of tea. No breakfast in the old
regime dismantling as sterling rose

like the sun. On the streets thick ice.
How did we solve the food conundrum?
In the building of the Soviet Writers Union

we were greeted by Yevtushenko: *Well done.*
The dawn of glasnost and perestroika
melting in the forecourts, alleys

and grand boulevards, unheeded by the throng
of poets trading on the floor of the Union.
At minus 24 the capital slipped into oblivion.

Our entrée to lunch was *prix fixé*
two bottles of vodka from the batch

purloined under dark arches. All we heard
was *chink chink* as our £s were counted.
Commodities offered by our chau££eur

who learnt the art of barter & exchange
in a heart's breath. I was thinking in the language
of food. Moscow in the snow was a frozen forest

of arrested intentions. At the end of the corridor
the eternal samovar was in charge.

II

Wolves of snow chased our train from Petersburg
to the crystal cold heart of Moscow. Our chauffeur shrugs
to our enquiry about chains on tyres. The polished
road gleams like alabaster.
                          Poets live dangerously
chinking glasses with illicit vodka. The avant-garde
la crème de la crème   offer us boiled potatoes
traditional staple with Russian suicidal gestures
of down-in-one.   We decamp into Metro gilded palaces
with echoes of Xanadu.   Price of entrée: *a kopek*.

Travellers, poets, partygoers rally to the flag
of Bohemia.   The romance of the bird
set free   breaking the bones of the chest.

In a high up apartment   falling in love
obligatory   poets on their knees after toasts
a reveller announces he will give up everything
for poetry.   In his sealed car with dark windows
    he says he's in Government
the Economics Minister
his car gliding silently like a sleigh in a fairy story.

It's in the English papers when we get home
    his resignation.   In the tissue thin books all
our signatures   a declaration.

III

My friend is freezing under his ex-Navy coat
fashionable in the Seventies. I'm warm in ancient fur
I stitch up each evening like Penelope at the loom.

On the Old Arbat a glint of gold and amber earrings.
It's way below old Zero. Russians rub their noses
at us as they pass   like cars flashing at the unlit jalopy.

In the café without food there are radiators and mud.
It is healthily warm. We have solved the food conundrum.
At the Writers Union we tout our vodka   old hands.

We edge onto the ice of mercantile habits.

State rationing   two bottles per citizen   our ace.

The hotels dredge up chicken croquettes
in name only   inside the shell a white slime.
Waiters with nothing to do open jackets

with hidden linings of cheap goods   the same
empty casket. Last time in Moscow tables
of yoghurt and caviar and Red champagne.

It was summer. The mild breeze of perestroika
    poets out of the closet   hope and bitterness
poured with vodka laced with orange berries.

We tasted fresh food and fresh ideals over in a flash.

The Interregnum. At the end of the corridor
the samovar presides.   No one listens
to Cassandra   the red flag
lowered like a rag   sunrise to sunset.
The long night has surprises.

IV

We sat in splendour in ex-Leningrad   the last supper
while the flag was red   a circle of hungry poets

brought to the table by visitors. Price of entrée: *livres*
to be precise, the currency *a la mode* for food,

1 Rouble to the £ dropped to 130 in one flight.
At the doors of the *Café Litterateur*   clicking heels

hands kissed in old Tsarist manners   Pushkin's last
breakfast before his duel   something so sacred

can't be changed by regimes   overarching silver trees
between tables   poets with privileges like money

shown to a private room   set with silver and Pepsi Cola
unchanging St Petersburg grandeur   new brands

somehow in the room of never never land
sumptuous banquet of many courses   interlaced

with musical interludes   for our ears only
in set aside rooms   opera singers and pianists hired

for our party   we trouped dutifully to listen
old Russia had never melted   old ice uncracked

Red Calvary lost in the snow
the old White monocles on show   poets serenaded.

Fine food a spectacle   the waiters brought our bill
like a scene from Chekhov   to the nouveau riche.

Peter and I   presiding   beggars at the feast
unaccustomed to the gesture   grandly paid for all

£2.50 per head   cheap at the price   we thought of Pushkin
who paid dearly after breakfast   the Leningrad poets

had a right to sit at his table.

V

We were looking for *The People of the Night*
price of entry circa 1987: a whisper
the summons had come   lunch in the tower block
a tin of peas   a rose tinted cake.

Artists/poets/sculptors   100 strong
the tower block swayed (*it didn't*)   emotions
ran out into the street   the *avant garde*
was bristling   dual poems   dual thoughts   duel.

Vladimir Druk led his troops   the capital shook (*it didn't*)
explosions of poetry in the street   Moscow
alight   Druk's black and white book.

Poems changed hands   the currency
of perestroika.   At the doors of the Kremlin
we were stopped   the shoes of one visitor
were trainers.   *Who are you?* (the guard

of the fortress)   *Poets.   Prove it!*
The offender recites *Ozymandias.*
The guard nods   *Shelley*   the password.
It is summer   the thaw   pages are snow

and fierce frost   the pages of winter
stiff with words   the leaves of grass
iceladen   the leaves tremble
we drink vodka into the night laced

with bright orange berries   *Novy Mir*
raises its flag of sedition   Oleg Chukhontsev
held the tiller   there was the past
and the future   with no rest in between.

The dead have no fear   the poems of the dead
awoke   the poems of the living ran barefoot.
We talked into the night   the night
ached with meaning   the summer was fading

before we knew it.   I hold in my hand
The Poetry of Perestroika   the entente cordial
between poets   smoke and mirrors
The People of the Night smashed the glass

everyone lit a cigarette.

VI

We stood at the statute of Peter the Great
    in the market for fur hats   he was fat
it must be our man   his coat a dome
of concealment.

With wintry prospects we chose without question
the forbidden headgear everyone was wearing
black fur with flaps.   Illicit like vodka
sellers cruising like seagulls around the statue.

Petersburg a warren of grand streets   doors
high as giants   our pockets stuffed with tenners
like to££s in Dandy cartoons   in the gloom
of December (dark at 2) price of entry:
£10 token fee per poem   now gold

to hand over for gifts of language.

We creep up cold lit stairs
to the modest flat of Elena Shvarts
the pale faced poet who never eats
(not something we witnessed at meals).

(her Eurydice pleads with the last touch
of rosy nails)

Her poem at the fall of the rouble
   rose in the world of numbers & assets & finance.

Elena lit her signature cigarette

   her windfall in her pocket.

She writes in gestures
where betrayal is significant

the price of entry to hell: heaven.

VII Coda: The Blue Stuff

Alone in the hideaway we had breakfast. Three poets alone.
A breakfast of yogurt and the blue stuff, a sparkling
blue cordial, and echoing silence from the empty hall.

Solitary in Soviet Asia and we talked of marketing
the blue stuff to the world, the talk of poets without skill

in the buying and selling department. Our advice free
at the point of delivery for Tashkent merchants
who lacked global competence, their ancient lorries

clapped-out and struggling on perestroika highways,
now unguarded, like this compound in back streets.

No one to salute us at the steel gates. No other guests.
Once kept for the Party we were told. A secret place.
We stayed a couple of days, lodging in the left over

1960s rooms conspicuous by their lack of identity
and general emptiness. The limousine came for us.

The highlight was breakfast. On the table the blue cordial
sparkling in its bottles. Blue as ink, impossibly blue.
A drink from the Arabian Nights. A thousand nights

and a thousand stories. It was the drink to rival Cola.
It was 1987 and the genie was out of the bottle.

Kin

Fosse Way

for Gillian Allnutt   ·

Childhood pavement.
   Midlands causeway.

On my bicycle
the primrose woods
bluebells violets
cowslips on lane banks

   the war at my back.

Never the same number
the Rollright Stones
legend passed down
in the child's code book.

The wolds cross borders.
The shires woven ribbon.

   We wait for the sun
to break through in Durham

   my displacement.

I made my home in the valley
on the pilgrims' way

where priests prayed
in Maiden Bower, knelt
on the site with banners
as Scots were butchered.

Fosse, language for Bede's
burial, a ditch, a pathway.

Custom comes for me

touching no town
between Stowe and Leicester

crosses Warwickshire
like the traceline in my palm.

Half my mother's ashes
cast by Harbury windmill

stopped arms mark the spot.

We walk up from the Fosse
to lay what the wind distills

the clouds of dust and grit
lay on air   her essence.

Ode to Brummagem

The slow train to Birmingham
past Acocks Green to Snow Hill

in a single carriage to ourselves
on our way to Nanna's and her grand

walnut clock chiming quarters and hours
the clock now silent on my shelf.

All I have left of aunts building
sandwiches, plates carried to the lounge

like trophies, accompanied by
lighting up cigarettes and packets

thrown across to laps as if to say
catch it! and Nanna presiding

over her girls like a stately galleon
in the full sail of her full bosomed

pinafore, her hair like a bonnet
in iron rows of curls, and her arms

like a boxer's ready to strangle
the piano with thumps into Blue Moon.

The train to Birmingham stops
at all stations, mother and daughter

entering the necklace of the city,
low bridges, tunnels and lines

branching into junctions and sidings,
the signals dropping their arms

to the smell of work in the dark glades
of streets, tall stacks like a thicket

in the gloom, the aroma of soot, smoke
and steam wrapped her in a blanket.

Russell Terrace

On days of Dunkirk the appeal came by radio to invite into

homes the dazed soldiers. My mother and aunt walked up
the Parade and brought back a dozen wandering without units,

my father had a bad heart and could not fight. I remember
our front room packed with many heads and rough khaki,

whisky and smoke from cigarettes that thickened a blanket
of comfort, the blue haze like battle smoke which was a haven;

the men were adrift on the Parade, without purpose or compass,
as if by habit once in courtship, up and down the grand curve

of the street, now the path of aimless soldiers, some bandaged;
there were sandwiches, the clinking of teacups and sugar bowl.

I wasn't four and the story was told during the war by my father.

Leamington Spa 1940

Reparations

Reparations post war / not enough frocks / one for Sunday best /
she would parade in the park / not run / parents correctly a pace
behind / her hair in a pageboy / stiff as plaster / curling irons
torture / Sunday smell of tongs on paper / singed brown / smoke
uncoiling / at 11 declared I'll *never* give up wearing socks

/ In the tunnel she would hoot / somehow allowed / the echo
delicious as cold water / the long walk to Victoria Park / the Rec
in the week / girls on swings rock in little waves of invitation /
boys at a distance / swings chaperone talk / When she gave up
socks a boy cycled up the street / her aunt's at Russell Terrace /

cycled and circled / Auntie Bel at the window / Someone for you
/ On Victorian steps she was a maid / he glided like a skater
to a standstill / at her feet / steps chaperone talk / looking on /
she knew him / Would she go out with him? / He was 14 like her
/ unlike her he left school / for work / shy and fair haired

and handsome / Yes she said / He wrote her a note / showed off
to friends / the pencil rubbed out here and there / her corrections
/ her education 11 plus / his council school / he was courteous /
rowed her on the river / boats were formal statements of love /
the girl in the prow / the boy at the stern / chaperoned / She kept

the note / her first boyfriend Geoff Bolds / no-one can claim
his place / no-one rub out / his courtship / kindness / fair looks /
nothing but memory can restore the note / nothing but shame
remove her corrections / keep his plight of troth / in his own
words / stumbling script / halting first steps / the heart's poem.

The Stone Fights

stones
    thrown up
        lobbed in air
           a perfect arc
              to land onto heads
                of advancing children

                    enemy lines pitching stones
                  practising warfare playing
                    soldiers who went over the top cold
                    into the fire the bombardment

                    playing Agincourt arrows

                    we were at war our street
                  against theirs almost
                knightly almost
              dumb the rules
            of the

              game

Cupboard

Captured, boys' hands on her wrists, clammy,
leading her into the half-house on the estate
waiting for windows, waiting for the war to end.
Open thresholds, but cupboards in rooms. Sand
heaps left outside. The boys tugged on her hands.
They didn't know what to do with her, took
her to a cupboard. She smelt their sweat
the boys not particularly clean, earthy.
Fear smells raw, not hers, theirs. Something
was required after the chase, they shut her
into the cupboard, shut the door, that
sorted it, whatever was in the years beyond.

When everything went quiet, she let herself out.

Made in Birmingham

Darkness descends on the heads of Brummies
and their washing lines. Attention was paid
in the passage of buses through slums, the smell
of gas, it had to go post-war, she with her sense
of clearance and sweeping of paths, mowing
of lawns in Leamington, jobs for girls along
with a note to the library for romantic fiction
and errands to the butcher with coupons.
She is ready with her duster and broom.

The slums trouble her. Journey to the shops
through Saltley, a ring of gasworks and fumes
and Brum's towers, stacks, masts, trailing
volcanic plumes as if lit by hand to a cigarette,
long streets of factories and tenements,
bombarded by dirt, shovelled from the sky.
Smoke lifting itself to heaven from hearths
and hanging its net curtain at the window.
The bus conductor chimes his ticket machine
with the endearment *Duck*. She was changed

into a warrior. She tells no-one, not her mother
on the bus nor Nanna in the works canteen
smashing lumpen potatoes with a gadget.
Nor her laughing Brummie aunts and Janet,
the youngest who stammered and felt hard done.
She vanished into the family. No-one told her off
or what to do. At home in Leamington
there is a regime of obedience to the letter
and of punishment locked in the coal shed,
the chimney darkness of the gloom, iron smell
of coal, sitting on sharp lumps unbroken.

It kept her good, her father said. A model child.
He was wrong. Waiting for the latch to open,
the thin line of light from the door, in her mind
empty of persuasion, she was a changeling.
He went up in the world, became a Tory
and bought a house with gardens and a bay.
Wanted her to join the tennis club *at least*.
But she has debts to pay and vows to keep,
Saltley was on her long list. She enters her Brummie
room with no locks and curbs and forgot to shut
the door. She tidied up and became a Communist.

Whisky

The Black & White cat placed in time. Named
after a brand once famous. Her cat but not

her cat. He began to soil the home and beatings
did not improve the practice, flashback to

kittenhood and the cat nose pushed into the
puddle and the hit descending like a sword.

The cat was sent to the vet for his own good.
Something was wrong, something was ailing.

To be put down. Whisky disappeared and the blow
fell on her, the hard hit at the table for the wrong

of the knife and fork not aligned together.
She was put in the coalshed and locked in by

the latch and she watched the lean line of light
waiting for the latch to be lifted, the door open.

She sat on large coals, sharp and brilliant, and
there was more coal stored under an outside

tarpaulin. Here the cat sat one morning, the cat
had come back. Her Whisky like a miracle of

resurrection. But he would not move and enter
the house. All her stroking could not entice him,

sat like a sphinx. The riddle was how he returned
from the vet, the mystery not cleared up by

her father, the reproach of the cat on the coals
who was not purring. One day the cat left her

coal-sitting in the coalshed where stocks
were kept up and the hand still hit her and

the black vigil kept her good, she was told.

Liberty Hall

On the ridge my father stopped the car.
It was a favourite moment for us to view the smoke
flying like black ribbons from a benighted forest
of high stacks on the Birmingham plain.
'Truly awful,' said my father. At our feet were violets.
It was a kind of homecoming but we were free

of birthright, of the claims of ancestry, free
to be supervised in the company car.
I'm bidden to be quiet where violets
paused for safety on the brow of the smoke.
Warwickshire now entering the darkling plain,
losing crowns of hawthorn in the bald Forest

of Arden, leaf-fall of delicate soot, a new forest
sprung up with factory glades and back lanes free
of fresh air, but the call to arms was plain,
a family council and I'm still carsick back in the car,
my father and mother bringing their own smoke,
his pipe and her cigs and picked violets

for my Nan, the council in her lounge, the violets
in a jug. 'Now girls,' said my Nan, the avenging forest
in her chest, 'I'm getting on,' wreathed in smoke
from handed out cigs. Her life after the canteen, free
of smashing up spuds, she was starting up like a car
on the hill. 'I want to make it plain.

It's over to you.' The girls in turbans and curlers, plain
afternoon workwear, nodded like the heads of violets
in a draught. My father: 'I need to get back to the car.
Battery draining.' Cars were tended like forest
saplings with jugs of water and warming of plugs free
of their housing. The interlude was chance for a smoke.

'You just sit back Mom,' said Stella, an afterplume of smoke
curling from a hand uplifted. 'It's *toime,'* said in plain
Brummie, like a cymbal in a symphony, the free
chime of my family, wondrous as the violets
in the woods, the chime of this afternoon, plain
as my preference to be here as he came from the car.

In a cloud of pipe smoke beauty drained from the violets,
his temper was plain as the trees in the forest,
the lack of free air as we're ordered back to the car.

Errata

How they worked, my ancestors,
no pause of wealth or rest.
I sit here, descendant,
poet, they appear like ghosts
in strata after wearing of years.
My father's father and his father,
hewers in pits of the earth,
crossing the nineteenth century
with lamps ready for the blowout.

Lineage in darkness waiting
to crack the carapace.
He left the mine, J W Litherland,
and set his name above his sign,
Coalman. His son lifted from the dark
and into ambition, tool maker,
night school engineer, one
who loved perfection of the *'thou'*

and from his child, the action
of a lathe. No mistakes allowed.
I had been told how to behave.
From the darkness came blows
handed
down
and I was locked in the coal shed
unaware of perfection owed
to forebears and the gift
of the latch lifted on the dark,
above ground, and into the light.

What was given was rebellion,
a fallen angel from the patrimony,
and a love of open land with dells
and lanes, spinneys and copses,
a love of wildflowers, of the holy
county Warwickshire and cricket,
everything not below ground,
and the perfection of the *'thou'*
as I edit,
hand
down
the book unmarred by *Errata*.

Dream

Back in my home become cold and dark
the frontage opened up like a wound.

In the doorwell stood two coalmen
smelling of soot, the reek of soot,
come to take the age-old soot from
the departed house, a cleansing
of the deposit of chimneys sunk in a pit;

and an old bound book left on the shelf.
'We take anything.' A book of learning
with an ancient spine; the collection
the final rite of the abandoned home.

I let them in, the ancestors

to close accounts, my father's father
and his father before him. They were strong,

out of the past, hewers and purveyors
of coal and the dust of coal clung to them.
The smell of soot was a furnace blast.
My ancestors did what they did best,

the century aroma of unwashed work
walked in with them to empty the pit.
'We'll take the book.' One last look.

They had come, my ancestors.

I knew from their shiny sweated faces
at my doorstep they had come from hard
labouring, coalmen in black aprons,

to empty the house pit of soot the years
had filled, the centuries of fires

in the hearth, the blackening smoke,
the house had to be cleansed of living
and nothing left. They were big men,

they did their work and took the book.

Wild

We twisted our stockings to shreds
on the night of the party, tendrils
like jelly fish, the family gathering
in the flat over the shop, the same
record over and over *'twisting the night
away'*, it was pure breathless
silliness, cousins and aunts, sisters
brothers, we knew how to party.

Out came the deodorant from
Stella handed round for underarms,
that was all, the dawn came,
somebody was 21, the Brummie
clan dignified by 'The Family'
knew that husbands joined wives
under the matriarch Mother,
my Nanna, who gathered them
under ample arms and her
unappointed authority.

She moved through the crowd
like a sailing ship with right
of passage, her girls in tow,
she'd survived three husbands
two divorces and abandonment
by her lover, somehow collected
together the remnants by force
of gravity, her various homes
drew in the children and women
without fathers. She stood tall
and worked, kept by no-one.

She presided with a whisper
to each grandchild, *'I'll leave*
my rubyware to you.' Displayed
in the glass cabinet untouched.
Before she died we all went
to her highrise flat to celebrate
her Sixty Years. *'Over to you girls.'*
A special present was a glittering
marcasite necklace in the shape
of a tiara on a chain. After her party

we slept on the floor under coats
with laughter bubbling all through
the night with false cries of *'Quiet!'*
a soothing serenade of companions
with echoes of those shelters
in the war under the hum of planes
and insignia of Ack-Ack guns
and the *'Hush'!* to listen to bombs.
Her necklace is all I have left
and her unwound clock on my shelf.
And the inheritance. I'm always
the last to leave the party.

Givers

Roundel

It's about Jack, my name, a Brummie chain of father, grandfather
like a roundel, I slipped the link but Warwickshire tightened
the loveknot, what's handed on, certain voices, the *'toime'*
we all chimed, ambushed by what's missing, our past.
Auntie Janet with her stutter and fixed eye, lived in a high rise,
all Tile Cross at her window. On her doorstep a chicken or two.
She would tap her nose, not a word of the provenance,
she was just managing, getting by, would always get by,
in the world down the ladder, her humour complicit,
her flat a show piece of tidiness we violated with our teacups.
She would hover like a waitress impatient for new custom,
the only concern was to remove them from use, away
to the washing bowl for cleansing and back behind glass.
It was her turn to entertain, the sound of her voice would sink
and swim in Brummieness, an accent which pitched up and down
on a swelling sea, it should be protected forever, a homely voice,
a nod is as good as a wink voice, a voice never to be lost
or changed for small vowels, an irreverent voice, mischievous
and rule bending, a life below pomposity, a voice for Jack
the Lad, a voice of not toeing the line, of belonging, family.
*'What Oi've learnt in loife, is, you're oither a Taker or a Giver.
Oi'm a Giver.'* Tapping her chest. Announced with finality.

Rondo

A footballer when he was on the pitch, could not be heard,
but still the lips could be read for their Brummie home notes,
a footballer famous for his arms lifted like a dancer for balance,
his execution would travel like a waltz, then a jig, then a rondo,
preying on his pathway, an undeterred bee towards the blossom,
there's only his feet trapping and tapping, as he sways away
from those like brambles and thistles that would catch his shirt,
he is eloquent, licensed to speak with his feet in motion,
the ball like a secret not to be shared, not to be lost,
in his elegant solo on a crowded stage, the language seeking
its comma or full stop, the pass or delivery, Jack alone
tonight or tomorrow will twist and turn and pause, today
or another day and by him or another, the ball enter its doorway.

A Durham
Elegy

The Harrowing of the North

for Durham County Cricket Club

Winter skies over Durham. In the stratosphere
high winds stretch the clouds to thin scarves,
the moon in the bloom of a shawl, beneath
the long twilight, the heartbeat of the ground,
the shrouded wicket in hibernation, Kings bring
no gifts to lay on the turf on Twelfth Night,
the stable is empty of redemption, although
the evening star shines its solitaire diamond,
the ring of empty seats is not to be crowned.
The great cricket circle is that fairy ground
we do not trespass, sacred, holy, guarded
by the past, theatre of Albion's angels dressed
in white, a rite unconditional, fortress
of a treasure not to be bought or sold. Who
has entered the house and broken the hearth?
What vandal has clothed the air in despair?
The hearth goods ransacked. The empty seats
with no future. The Test lamp sentinels
with no switch. The embrace of the ground
is a widow without children. The vandals
entered without mercy. Struck down the pride
of Durham, put down the unarmed servants
in their quarters, the pennants were in tatters.
Sold off the warriors. Broke bonds of allegiance.
Men who are money Barons. They have no shame.
They are debt collectors. They scatter the village
and its green. They pillage what remains, the cups
looted from the cupboard. Mark them by their blows,
mark them by their words: This is a warning to others.
Eat grass. Eat the harshness of our deeds. Beg.

You are broken and defeated before the sun rises
and after the sun sets for five seasons by our reckoning,
shackled by our chains. Who will come to your aid?
We are dark lords. High winds racing above the earth
are turning clouds into scarves, the moon loses her shawl,
the ground is a shrine to the faithful, blessed by pilgrims.
Who will bring spear and sword? Jerusalem
was builded here among dark satanic mines.

January 2017

Brexit Wind

A cold wind from a cold coast,
the North Sea where foghorns
bleat like lost sheep. The fret

will tendril its way to Pennine
hills, over the shivering rivers
and the closed doors of the street.

From one windy village to another,
where high streets are just a row
on the brow, everything extracted

that looks like work, the decline
of towns that slip into harbours,
the once pretty villas uncared for

on the cliff edge. Unfinished
roads that wind through new
warehouse sheds to rusted

wire. You could understand
the depleted hope that never felt
austerity was anything but

punishment and the scorn of
a certain voice that called them
undeserving of the fat of the land

kept for those of certain income.
A cold wind from a cold coast,
a spiteful wind some would say,

a levelling wind that would bring
nothing but broken promises,
the kind they knew all about.

On The Eve of Brexit

Leaving England in such a sorry state where Lear
might lament, beggars have moved from hedgerows
to streets, the mad are mad again, their lunacy
without care, storms are breaking their high seas
on unprotected headlands and water meadows,
winds whistle and whine like fed up children,
not the time to be four score and foreshortened,
whatever is happening England is back on the heath,
turned out of doors by warring families to dwell
on unintended futures and calamity. *'Take
physic, pomp'*, the tablets are running out,
as the mad lead the blind to the cliff edge, no longer
metaphor, no longer a cultural symposium,
it never was, England cut in pieces again by greed
and pride, nothing comes of nothing like a fee
demanded, the interest compounded as if
there's always a price for everything, and love
not excepted, the overruled must speak for the ruled,
for it is he wrestling with conscience the poet
puts centre stage as the lightning conductor
of a broken country. Lear is about to die and regret
that surplus and penury were never to meet,
it's a history we are destined to repeat,
England full of disorders and closing borders,
answers which have tried and fail must try again,
the play warns the ending is not neat.
Death is the curtain but the tragedy is re-enacted,
the players move from generation to generation,
England failing in its treaties, failing its poor,
the young look on while we have wound ourselves
into our winding sheet, we did not save our fields,
nor our seas, nor our birds, nor our beasts,
the harvest spent like dirty money, no credit left.

Red Wall Down

I Heartlands

They didn't rise again. Fell away brick by brick.
Already worn they couldn't stand back to back.

And what came was emptiness. The closed mouths.

And they were kicking nothing about. On the coast
the wind blows sandpapery squalls and on hills
the mist clings to the side of the road. A landscape

of labour done. The heaps grassed over, what was
underground the marches and banners, the battle.

It's just a wasteland in the eye of the beholder.

Bitterness like the east wind chills to the bone.
Kicked as if they were nothing like old houses
to be pulled down, slate by slate and window

by window, as if marked for listing Category
D for demolition, the relics of Durham.

And when the disease would rise like Anarchy

they knew, the poor blighted villages, that Fraud
had come home to the abandoned heartlands.
And on the pale horse was the Minister for Fear.

II *Murton Colliery*

on the occasion of the 100th Gala

In the hush of dawn the band plays *Gresford*
for the loss of men and boys a dying fall.

The workings beneath their feet gave way.

On their banner 'Each for All'; the chairman
takes off his white cap as a signal.
In the hush of dawn the band plays *Gresford.*

The ground is riven with promises broken
fallen in faces and abandoned shale.

The workings beneath their feet gave way.

The banner sways on its ropes like a sail
marchers clapped at every gate and door.
In the hush of dawn they hear *Gresford.*

The future like a sinkhole was to take them all
the Lodge the Union and the pitmen.

The workings beneath their feet gave way.

An ill wind has a shrill declining call
days cut down into smaller pieces.
In the hush of dawn the dying fall of *Gresford.*

The workings beneath their feet gave way.

III **Winds**

On the second Saturday of July the bands
enter the waking city, the past enters early

into closed off streets, the drum like a warning,
a mourning drum, villagers come to mourn

their working lives. It's a refusal to comply.
Outside the County Hotel we hear *Gresford*.

The banner sways on its ropes like a sail.

This year the Gala will be dumb, struck dumb
as if Plague took pity on their pride and stopped

the masquerade, for how could they come
with banners and music to honour the dead

and comrades? They turned their backs.
Faced the other way. It wasn't a bitter wind

or unkind. It was the coming of the whirlwind.

~~The Big Meeting 2020~~

IV *Tides*

The sea returning to wash the coal shoreline,
dredges away the slag and shale, a century
of tipping over beaches the waste of the mine,
burnt umber strata in cliffs left behind, the lines
of buckets in constant motion now stopped.
The sea returning each tide for its haul.
The sea carries on its back the great load.

Under the coast the mine is creaking like a sail,

the tunnels buckling, the pit props breaking
under the stress of abandonment, pumps not
pumping, the sealed face with its locked down
coal, the mine is alive with sounds, emptiness
swallowing rock, the pitting of stones, water,
and roads once the haunt of pitmen inbye and
outbye are the property of the earth like a grave.

Ode on Gresford

'And the actual sun closed
Into what looks like a bible of coal'
Ted Hughes

Colliers all, worked out of sight of the sun.
Under their axes, in tubs, in the seams,

the coal winked its sunlight in the black
countering night under arches propped
at every yard, the only light their headbeams;
the slender shafts pinprick from afar,
from the tunnel's mouth, merely moving
like fireflies, ahead the low murmuring

of indistinct voices. Buried deep under tides,
they are detonating at the coal face,

in the mine where 13 died in the war safe
from bombs but not from firedamp breeding
deadly fumes, the explosion took them
all, those reading the bible of coal
as it came to hand, the location of text
which says the sun sends its fire laid down

between these rocks, this seam of carbon
packaged for earth. The coal says gifts

come with warnings, nothing is sacred
if taken without attention. There was no
reply from the dead. On these histories
the miners write their bible every time
they honour their own. They are fables
of those below ground digging for sunlight

and the spirit moved in the composer of
Gresford, a Durham miner Robert Saint,

by the fate of *two hundred & sixty-six*
at the Colliery disaster of that name.
And sacred his music became, the hymn
with a dying fall. For all who reflect
and mark respect, the music holds sunlight
of the lives closed in the bible of coal

and opens the book to read their names.

Gone in the Morning

The ex-coalfield worth a pittance, the winnings all done.
I'm not from here but tears are won for grief of Durham

and the living fire and bread, hearths of community,
the moors and the valleys in unison, bare of industry

passed over for new estates. The Vikings left the land
bloodsoaked and underground the workings by hand

were hard in tight seams, the black death in lungs,
and no one to hear above ground the coughing.

A closed book, the fells wrote a chapter of ghosts
left behind when tents which had landed like a host

of sheltering birds or sudden pitched army were all gone
one morning, the Lead no longer pickings to be won.

Ghosts you can hear whistling for work in the fog,
that was the fate of Coal in the valley, the shut up gob,

in the wilderness of ex-work, ex-miners, ex-Lodge men.
I came to the County at the time of the banner and Union.

The curlew laments on the fells, the seagulls in the valley,
the past with trappings, the spinning wheel like a jenny

carted off to the dump or Museums, not an echo behind,
not a song like *Wor Nan's a Mazer* in the sterile helm wind,

in the tongues of the young, they buried it with bitterness
under grass and wild flowers and without a cross.

What stays open is the wound, a flaying of the North East,
the waste washed away daily on the coal coast.

The curlew laments in the fells, the seagulls in the valley.
Black tears of the sand disappear as augury.

What lasts is but a sense of place and displacement.
In the vaults of the hills the lost sentiments.

For the soul of the County, for the mourning of the curlew,
let the silence break its committal, its vow.

For the moortops, for the sea, for seagulls crying in the valley,
let the silence speak, the silence in cages locked away.

I'm far from the kinship of my heartland but near
to the deeper absence of what was once here.

I owe my tears to the way of life of the winnings,
everything that mattered gone in the morning.

the winning: old term for coalmine; gob: gap left by extraction

Crows

The Approaching Storm

A grey interlude of calm and a whine
in the woods, a lone siren.
Diamonds arrive on my window,
tracery of casual beauty.
The grey overhang of cloud
tells us nothing, it's blank

like a liar avoiding a question.
Seeds of rain and a lone bird aloft
as if scouting. Winter trees twitch
and stir. Forerunners in runes
if we read signs like sea captains
in harbour. We wait for Storm Dennis,

an ambush of spiral galaxy arms
spinning clockwise in our waters.
We reap our harvest of CO_2
glued to our planet in an unkind
blanket. So the future is forecast
turning wind into a mill of isobars.

In the calm nothing has arrived.
Seagulls in the west will brave the worst.
The storm front touches the coast
in a brutal blow of weather we trusted.
As raindrops thicken like a rash
and weep like sores, like calligraphy.

Breath of the Virus

Frost on the lawn   retreating
before the spring sun. It says I'm
not substantial   I'm pencilled in.

The birds are at their happiest
courting in the sky   they
have time for it. Spring undeterred

by blight on humans   suffering
when disease is airborne
on the wing.   The fate

of the planet is arbitrary
the weak will go   and the strong.
The half   life of the virus

on the breath   pencil marks
of life pencilled in   a sketch
not quite finished   interrupted.

A half   soul seeks its page
to write, it's so old it has   no
thought except   commandment

to seed the earth   messenger
not the message   returning to
first days   stammering, stuttering

its incomplete   script
unlike the pen
which never stopped writing

the stumblings   of life
twist of   symmetry
the advent of the host   to be.

The Start of The Season

What is beauty but the arc
of the endeavour, mano a mano,
the courtliness and the defiance?

the raised bat and the click
before batsmen cross, what game
slows to the tempo of knitting

and yet each ball coveted,
the grandeur of the knee lowered
to the hauteur of the cover drive

stamped like a sovereign seal
on the afternoon and we all
murmur, *no need to run*

as the batsman holds the pose?
like a dancer after an arabesque,
for applause of the kind that greets

arias in operas, the batsman pauses,
adjusts his gloves twice, and squints
for the quick single that comes next.

March 2020

Isolation

for my four grandsons

The sky's flimsiest clouds could not be
fabricated, not by all the endeavours
of finest silks or muslins. High winds
had spun and re-spun countless threads
in gossamer of different weights.
The clouds' finesse free to all,
the skies empty of planes, *look up*

the moon is rising in a veil, nature
is grandstanding, the spring of no games,
no cricket, no whites on grass, sky
melodies of palest blue and gauze.
The trees are turning green, a fuzz
of spring, the trees like young men
in their step, the sap in their limbs,

like grandsons at Eastertide, like them.

Nostalgia

for Linda Saunders

Dear friend we can't undo the lockdown

of nostalgia. We were young when we met.
We walked through the garlic woods of Durham,
the white streams, swam in fissures between rocks

on the hills, walked our lives and our language

into memory like a cinema reel which starts
without warning; the projectionist
in the high up office has a cupboard full.

Deep moments pushed up from bare ground.

They were phantoms vanishing as they came
like the sirens over the trees to the hospital.
What we learn, the past will insist

that memories live in rooms quite apart.

Winchester

Streets unwove as we walked
                              medieval unwinding
to the cathedral heart, *the shop we entered,*

        I am wearing now the earrings
of rose quartz (like sweets in sucked roundness)

        I sought to pair with a favoured necklace
a bargain for a fiver
                              the one I never wear

    its clusters of rose quartz unliked, the pairing
too absolute. *Your pleasure in my find*

pins the moment   my unsought happiness
        at the chance of a match
                              blessed the day
of walking through cloisters
                              coming across
unknown cathedral quarters

the day returns as I pick pink globes encased
in silver, *your glee, your willingness*
                              to share a small joy
that expanded effortlessly.

What we keep and what we discard
                              is unknown.
The pairing did not last, but the day
in Winchester
                    stays encased in our friendship.
The day unwove
            as we looked into the window
the memory unwinding
                    to the heart's archive.

Upriver

I went back to the past where the past had moved on,
descending from bridge to waterfront, the day sunny,
the river rippling and gleaming on its way downstream.
A few echoes, *The Blue Anchor*, so we know where we are,
at Hammersmith Reach, the jetty and swinging boats,
memories should jostle but they're quiet where paths
collide and separate and two futures might have argued;

no contest at all, upriver was my home losing the flood,
the river heading towards the sea not looking back,
the barge constrained by chains wanting to sail from
moorings, an old lamp on a hook the relic of merchant
days, now bereft of the means, conversion hauling down
its beauty like cutting off long hair, the tawny sails
now a fiction, the decks were bare like a shaved head.

At morning birds would fly upriver, swans and geese
honking to rise in long laboured take-off, pressing above
the breast of the water, heavy-winged; small boats follow,
panting with wheezy engines, one we called the dog boat,
and the river police patrolling in motorcraft with a beat
like a heartbeat, the river tide racing one way or another
until that pause of hesitation, dead water time, musing

and milling, half hour of safety, slack water intermission
but tides turn and run and brace the water like decisions.
I walk upriver, it's old ground, past *The Dove* but then step
inside the ancient tavern, somehow a backdrop for lovers,
hoping to impress with its deep history and low lighting,
it's like a secret not well kept, a secluded place for meetings
beginning or ending, or like dead water, nothing happening.

I leave an empty place for ghosts to sit. The past is closed
and all the chaos of unhappiness is put to bed, such a walk
retraces steps without awakening anxiety or pain, we are all
companions of the same moment whether alive or dead;
and here I am at *St Peter's Wharf* or where it used to be
behind the door hidden in the wall, the quick path through
the yard to the secret exposure of three barges tied together,

moving in motion like heavy matrons arm in arm with broad
beams cast adrift on the chime of the water, rocking them
from side to side, the *Orwell* with gangplank over the brink –
the ownership of stepping on board, a river welcome from
dank air, muddy foreshores, steep banks and only the water ebbs,
the scent arising from a deep well, damp concrete smell
of air raid shelters and paraffin stove. The smell of safety.

I walk on. The tide is out. The *Eyot* no longer an island, pebbles
and mud underfoot we trod here and after your funeral I carried
my flowers to the spot closest to our mooring and threw them
on the water as it fled, knew they would journey lower and lower.
I learnt your brother, under instruction to leave your ashes
to the garden of remembrance, came here by the river edge
and threw them on the same tide and nothing consoles me

more, it is a kind of forgiveness, the only kind I am allowed.

Anniversary

for Barry, 9 May 2020

I know I've *gone over* like the flowers.

The skin tiring of the effort, the flesh
for holding up, why bother? the years

fret with the mind still young.
We use metaphors of the incoming
tide but it's more the departing sea

on the flat sands of the coastline,
the miles and miles of rippled beach

and the stretch to the sea out of reach.

I know I've *gone over* like the flowers
the Greek moment of apoptosis,
the dropping of petals, the crisis.

These thoughts in isolation in the wake
of your interrupted life, if not by choice,

your inclination to die mid song,
to not rehearse decline, the sea's retreat,
and keep the waves still at your feet,

not to be here, elderly and unfit,
the miles and miles of crippled beach,

not to hear the sea with shells of talk.

The sky / a wrap of pearl grey and pink silk.

Alliums in the Rain

Unbeaten down you were stark seed heads in elderly frames,
overnight rain frilled spikes to pink spangled net, alliums,

queens of the border, your net balls starburst not dust,
preen like girls in party frocks. Rain strung a thousand sequins

like a thousand stories in autumn brains, your crowned
thoughts sparkle, allium cages of spent flowers just washed

flourish a pink rinse, like girls again in their heads, memories
caught in the rain, the old with their caps of sequences.

The Gardener's Counsel

I allow the garden to die. Crusted stems of seedheads
spear the border. The plants compete in dishevelling;
daises like dying suns reduced to hard little beads
without coronas of petals. They're frail and wither

within sprays of self-setting tiny blue flowers now
sparse. The floret red roses have refused to fade and
deepen like sunken rouge. The garden has final shows

of romance, outvying neatness; yarrow blown by winds,
high wands of gold emblems, some bent at the knees,
and there is one immaculate rose with divine scent,
a latecomer to the party still murmuring in dust

spillage under bushes thinking of leaving; August
is her moment of entry on the stage; the ragged
and the blowsy on their last drinks. I allow truth.

The seasons, the heat, the rain, have stained the garden;
plants lean on neighbours, there are graves for the unborn,
they weave a web, every day they are constantly edited,
a leaf here, petal fall, and autumn flowers in abeyance.

I am ahead. In my limbs winter resides, weakness creeps
and overmasters rest. The winter garden will not sleep,
it is a fortress of iron, a barricade, a promise, a bridge,

I am asking myself to climb this scree to the ridge
where I can see Easter, a pink flush over winter trees
as we pass the equinox to intimations of green
barely sketched in branches, the garden full of daffodils.

Forget summer is shedding petals, seedheads like skulls.

I am here in the daffodil garden. The lawn crystalline.

A Ghazal for Ian Bell

A long walk off at Cardiff, you have to keep walking.
    The game is over, the long game, Bell kept walking.

The artist is alone, the field was his wide canvas,
    he leaves behind his motifs of beauty by walking.

Each day the game closes, players together gather,
    success and failure are left on the field by walking.

In the mind of one, the days have come to an end
    the days of scripture, the days of stories, in walking.

At his back the players pause at the field's edge,
    in the wake of a single line, applaud his lone walking.

Dead battles lie in the grass, he led himself away.
    His song is sung but to the refrain of walking.

Silence was the backdrop, silence in the stands,
    eloquent were petals of applause to the man walking.

The blade master with his bat, cold in the hand,
    looks ahead, his art put aside on walking.

Spring returns, but not the wingbeat of his willow
    with the swallows, summer departs with his walking.

September 2020: no spectators permitted

Elegy

after Atrodyssey by Siegfried Zademack

Muses line up in chorus, for this is theatre or a backcloth
to opera, and No-one is tied to a chair and forced to listen.

Irony the only comment, irony swinging from the sky
like a lead weight. The scroll empty of the wine and the rose.

The viaduct steps over the city floored at its feet, the trees
are like chess pieces, the city a board game *aka* Monopoly

so well named, and players risk their counterfeit money.
Listen! It could be roulette or blackjack, throw the dice

for the city, the cards are falling from the sky. The black
crow is solitary on the lawn. Birds are shifting in chorus

like ideograms. Time to read the script in the scriptures.
The dying city picked over by plunderers like Vikings.

The little terraces in side streets, in the district of striding
arches, windows frame their souls in purgatory, unattended

by the patron saint immobile in the cathedral. Durham
no longer a fortress, no one praying in Maiden Bower.

And litter in the gutter backs up like fluttering birds
seizing the moment to fly, rats nest in yards, the summer

silence hangs over the ghost city, where did everyone go?
when did they leave? When autumn comes and swallows

depart, the tide turns and this time they will not be alone.
Untenanted homes will be tenanted for another year

in the girdle of unlidded bins, the overgrown gardens,
the unwashed windows, the minimum fuss, the disease

doesn't mind overcrowded rooms, fetid air, lack of brooms!
Welcome! to the city abandoned by its guardians, those

guardians on the hill who failed to look down, no statues
to them, no plaques, no garlands, no days of wine and roses,

dealers who marked the deck, sold the city under their feet
without a handshake, with a nod over the heads of citizens.

For this is theatre or opera or a crystal ball, Durham a sign
of things to come, a metaphor of fate unguarded where

consequences flow like detritus, where failure was a lack
of care and laissez-faire a horizon gone over the hill.

Irony a lone bell, a cathedral bell tolling on a single note,
like an elegy. All bets are off. *Les Jeux Sont Faits.*

Memento Mori

a conversation for Diane Cockburn

We were walking through the last month of autumn,

the sky a shining blue, no wind but little rills of cold
on our faces, the view was a strange assembly
of theatrical cut-outs with such a depth of focus

that the trees and grasses looked placed there
in dimensions of the hillside, the prickles
on scissorsharp stalks, everything cut precisely,
no blurred lines, no softening the grit of seeds,

the spikes of gorse, autumnal brittleness.

You share rock cakes on a bench and the sea of grass
brimmed without murmur to trees, bushes, footpath.
We were climbing to a height where a man sits

made of wicker, his legs in poor shape. He wears
a cap and muffler. He rests and we rest, he needs
attention, left out in all weathers, a crumpled man,
his decay our decay, all around is dying back.

Over there, lying in the grass, is his counterpart,

a young man who is alive and reading a book.
We call across, *What are you reading?* He holds it up:
Poetry. He has settled in the long grass off the path,

where grass is damp. The young poet is holding a lamp,
the lamp of poetry, here in the windless autumn day
with cold ripples and air like mountain water, and sky
blue as earth's girdle in space, the blue of earth's bloom.

We're poets, we tell him and talk of Shelley's poem

Julian and Maddelo. A conversation with Byron
and a visit to a madman who had loved and lost.
Shelley did not heed his friend's advice: *If you can't swim,*

beware of Providence. Everywhere Memento Mori
but poetry is as permanent as the grass, the life blades.

Allusions

The gorse looks winter dead. On the hillside jagged bushes.
My friend is searching their carcases. *They never stop flowering,*

there is always a flower in winter. The bushes denied this,

rank on rank of ragged prickles. *Gorse is favoured by fairies*
you insist. *Look!* High up one yellow bud like a tiny buoy

on a murky sea marking the flowering. Through wires

and antennae a thread of sap. The bush keeps one bud alight
like a shrug of the exhausted mother or the eyelids

of Gordon Hodgeon blinking his poetry to nurses.
The gorse looks winter dead. Inside his head the poems hid.

They never stopped flowering. The bush keeps alight one bud.

We were walking in our lockdown, the year of remote living like
a blight of aloneness. Allusions rise up to greet me, vanish

as quickly as the fairies. I welcome the brambles, thickets

and thistles clasping my coat, the jagged gorse no one could
push through, evidence of resistance, impervious, flowering.

For The Forlorn

Clouds are familiars
funnelling grey-backed out of the sky,
   come to the shore of the window.

The uncontrollable moment

when depression left the room
   (and waking up to it),
                     the cloud she carried,
               was outside
   in visible descending pirouettes.

The moment depression took on the *shape*
of billowing chimney smoke
   coiling back into the chimney,

her mind had lost the weather,
the overcast day,
   to the onset of something worse

      playing tricks.

~~Xmas 2020~~

In Abandoned Grounds

Evening light behind black trees and one bird
dark-winged glides across the beauty of winter.
I walk here through seasons, each bench enamelled
with a name. Art and war were housed together.
Benches left like tombstones in a graveyard.
A new housing estate will strip the scene
of memorials and the duck pond not spared.

Cold wind on New Year's Day, a dousing keen
air not to raise your hopes, keep them in place,
hands in pockets, head down, comfort from crows –
single black question marks stalk without grace
they ask for truth on a wildscape of grass.
The crow unfavoured by the world or word
is writing the script today as Corvid.

Former DLI Museum & Art Gallery, Durham

Arrival of Snow

I looked round from my notepaper,
                              flurries of snow
were thickly drifting
spending so much time
                              turning and twisting
released
        from the confinement of clouds,
hurling themselves   into air
                              chasing each other,
snow having such a happy time,
whiter than
this flat white page which seems
                              to lie senseless
under penmarks,
            the snow effortlessly erasing
the lawn into a plump
                    quilt tucked in at the edges.

The wind is driving the snow landing silently
on the garden and woods. The trees, marooned
ghosts,
        are islands lost in the snow haze,
                                    steadfast,
watching it all passively, snow conquering
the landscape
        like a death we might welcome,
gently burying us
                in cold time.
                              By evening snow
has stopped arriving. Everything
                              has a white ruff,
everything is silent, a hard frost lays its cold lips
to the bushes, each leaf with its cup of snow.

Elementary

No crows on the grass.
Ice pellets frail curtain
on the path tiny spheres

nature has no problem
with production line
of hail balls by the billion.

I tread on their shells
already dying water beads
cluster by the door

occupy the step as if
they have a choice a voice
elements learning to speak,

sighing in the wind conscious
of their short mayfly lives
their jelly fish shoals,

sudden virus blooming,
hailstones in a chorus
landing from the skies.

The grass their platform
identical scatterings
the pellets a fusillade.

Languages of Time

It was talking incessantly in its own language
at the race where a mill might have stood instead
of green banks, rough grass and crumbling mud edges,

but what gave the river grace
at this unkempt spot,

where beauty was in the water –
moving into runnels of light and dark twisting coils
and surges of spiralling vortices as if demonstrating
how the universe spins,

across the surfaces of the Wear, grace took the shape of antithesis,
sharp splints of countermovement, cutting and splicing air,

the raiding of swifts, unceasing, tiny darts puncturing and weaving
as if punching holes through the tapestry of landscape,
held our eyes, all lines of flight crisscrossing and just missing,

how did they evolve this daring
wire dance and water skimming without plummeting?

Scraps like metallic gizmos born of feather and lightness of bone
                                        write their verse
over the river of ancient chemistry
a confluence of arrows and flows

why air? why water? why grass? when did swifts appear?
Was this river engraved at the start of time

in the darting particles, in the spinning gases?
                            The swifts awaiting their chance?

Easter Tide

Light winds that chill, cold currents
lie over the land: Easterlies!

Flowers must wait in their beds
or caught in light apparel of buds.

Wet Morning After

The wet morning is not adventurous.
In the grass and flowers, it will not sigh,
it is remarkably still, sodden and reflective.

The purple strife is leaning with the weight
of raindrops as if overhearing the roses

but they are silent. In Durham Covid
is blooming among the young. I sit
in my glass house, out of the rain, away
from the seeding of the virus air-blown,

writing with my pen like a hypodermic
needle which pricked my arm twice.

I have bound together the yarrow thrice,
its stems spinning plates of yellow
like a scene from the Chinese Opera.

Precautionary! The gales are still
in the Channel. Our government doesn't
batten down hatches. Distrusts experts

with weather charts, scrolls of isobars
tightening and winding the wind
into a thumbprint and given a name.

Storms are an opportunity to sail close
to the wind, to the rocks, to the drowned.

Gardening and dying are the outlook.

My Mother's House

That The Moon

That the moon had such a tail, a coil
   of woven clouds stitched and pleated

the sky rippled like the sea silvery dark
    and restless, a night music of wakefulness.

     The moon crushed in a vortex of bars

     where moonlight gleamed
      intermittently. Each cloud was foam lit.

The sea an echo, never ceasing

  undertone of shuffling suggestions,
   how to escape how to talk out of a corner

    the sky an illusion of sort
      ripples streamed to the horizon faint
       Jupiter in a net and the full moon

     shrugging fleece around its shoulders

     like a Russian tsar on the steppes

    not showing his face to the populace.

The moon rose clear like a queen
    the huntress not to be caught or held.

Free
yet chained to the sea
       by invisible ties not chosen.
Empress of the sky or just a woman.

August, Es Carregador, Mallorca, 2021

Inspired by Birds

The far field
raucous geesebabble.
They'll be gone today or tomorrow
over cloud at high altitude where resistance is thin
each one beautiful as Concorde. The plane a dart above
shoals of birds, banks to camber at the charcoal edge of space
and nothing vibrates not even a coin standing on end in the cabin.

The silent
flight untiring birds
would envy. We knew the wonder of
birds, that thrill, that magic. On my keyring a new
silver chevron. Waiting in a queue at an airport in the US
on Amber, my keys were spotted on a tray. *Let them through!*
They have flown on Concorde! All eyes skyward to the white bird.

Jacqueline

High line of Acton from my window
Chiswick Empire spinning ball
the nights of roofs / days of attic living

could be Paris / Jean Paul Sartre open at my table
grainy coffee / a zigzag of wallpapers
intentionally breaking every rule

and calmly surveying the new order
a portrait by Picasso
presiding over passion

primary colours of red and blue
still presides in my home.
I didn't know her name was mine.

She survives two fires and a flood
my two marriages
the to-ing and fro-ing of partners

and two years of the echoing
emptiness of Covid as we look over
the end of the bed together

over the deep Vale of trees
over the balcony doors and rail
over a settled stillness behind glass

she turns her head aslant / her hands folded
and wrapped one over the other
she was his last wife / survived the mistresses.

She was my youth and womanhood.
The Roads to Freedom my textbook
and newly acquired Party Card as proof

no half measures / but nothing cut and dried
the *avant garde* the angel on my shoulder.
I would always be on the outside, untied.

In Times of Storms

Not the first storm which took the fences away dancing in the wind
like flotsam, it was the second, not the forerunner, it was the gusts
of the many fingered Malik, not the decoy, but the pickpocket.

The garden was shriven, ripped of its defences, an open wound,
exposed to the world the intimate chairs, the unpainted bench,
the top heavy parasol bought for its canopy, laid aside, propped

by the downpipe, the immovable iron table sent from Germany
with its lacy patterns, smaller than it looked on the website,
on display with two rattan chairs made to last in all weathers.

They were the ones to heel over. Fences make good neighbours
who want a share in the wreckage. Like a grandee I insist
on my privilege to bear cost. They wave away my claims,

wave them away as if they were small beer. We rise up in storms
as if manning the barricades, ancient blood awake in our veins,
villeins and serfs, peasants and yeomen, all hands to the pump,

all hands to the plough, the harvest, the flood, the forest fire,
excited to find the commons alive, share in the war effort
and forget ourselves for a while, storms unpick us and test fear,

but there is glory in dismay, the ravaged roof, a poetic disorder
in the heap of slates, the surprised attic, the intimate contents
of things no longer wanted. The worst of the blitz was the bomb

struck houses and the naked staircases like ladders in stockings.
Storms have names like Arwen and Malik but there is no such thing
as a pet storm, they flew over the oceans at breath height and grew.

The Fragile Lives of Footballers

They have lives of plus or minus. The flowers all picked
every week. Strewn around with broken stems or garlanded.
Formations in their heads before they sleep.
Days ending with a heavy heart
or a light heart. Playing for England they look into a chasm.
A nation is watching. A world is watching.

The performance waits to be opened like a book. Unlike a book
it is not reliving the past. It flows with time. They are running
in the invisible sea of time, choices weigh on their feet.
Pressing on their heels the web of ghost moves:
woven and unwoven, chosen and not chosen,

and their counterparts intercept their path, undo and interrupt
the sea of thoughts. Pick up the thread, start again.
They are carrying each other like a tired army wave on wave
of cresting the hill and milling, the ball a signal /
running into the thicket / the one chance / may fall at their feet.

Time is a forking path. Luck changes sides.
The game is a jigsaw shaken apart.

The ball echoing the fabric of the lifestream,
how it flows from our loom as they weave and unweave
success and failure, all outcomes as a matrix.
The world is watching their mastery / half won /
half lost / initiates our souls into the mystery of mistakes /

the thread is knotted when the thread breaks.

The Valley of Thorns

Gardens always have temporary status.
Look away and the thickets have joined hands
in the land of unguarded moments. *Is this garden yours?*

Prevent your children from destroying it!
There is no need to keep checking on thorns
building VISA gates, Entry and Exit signs,
slights with needle leaves, and where you might

have walked a line appears like a line drawn in the sand
and it is harder to cross than swallow.

Territory is a war of silence devoid of birdsong.

I have come to this place of old age
with the child who hands on the baton.

The wartime of Warwickshire, the cowslip banks,
little whittled boats jostling to reach the pond,
nettle ditches she jumped over, the red maythorn.

At home she was locked in the coalshed *for her own good.*
Acrid smell of slack waiting for the door to unlatch.
A line of light is glowing above the door like neon.

A vow like a walled garden.

England with its vanished vistas.

Thoughts on Mothering Sunday

In Memoriam

Lilies arch, they won't survive their vases, like meadow flowers
I picked as a daughter, wilting in jamjars on window ledges.

Except when pressed between these pages.

My garden is alight with lamps of daffodils. I take the woodland
path. My past house without light, empty of all it held.

No one to stand outside and grieve like Troilus

for Crysede, her house is vacant like mine. To note the tidal
dirt over windows, primroses buried in five years of leaves,

cut down magnolia, cut down wisteria

that wound around the balcony. The mischief of neglect,
the rotting of frames, unloved back yard, unpainted frontage,

a student house which has lost its gate.

For Tennyson dispossessed in the rain, the house is empty
on the street, in the bald morning on the blank day. Walk.

Except the house stays in the mind in the dark.

On Entering *Madroño*

for my daughter and son, Rachel and Ben

Entering my mother's house, my father's house.

They came here to build in the sun, in island breezes,
my father *out of breath / lives / chances* oversees
Madroño rising from rocks, his redoubt / lookout.
Within, music and paintings, glint of glass, gather
under the soft light allowed by omission of power,
every day my mother handpumps water from below.

> *Consent from the sea, the sea knew our summer time,*
> *the cormorant fishing in the waters, dredged pebbles*
> *and seaweed, the small birds who sew the sky at dawn.*

Here I am late. The dried up land, withering lemon tree,

wisps of straw like old hair, thinning of time and ageing.
Through a locked door my children enter the past.
The long arch, the deep windows, what we thought lost.
My son cries in the kitchen alone. Her spirit in every room,
in her gate-legged table, safe in my home, she carried
overseas / *the oak sheen / the only reminder of England.*

I see it standing there between terrace and portal.

> *When we trod the path in half light to the sunrise*
> *strewn on water, the sea knew we would one day enter*
> *the house of my mother and the coast would assent.*

August, Sa Coma de ses Beyes, Mallorca, 2022

That the Sun

should be strong, the cicadas raise their din, the buzzsaws
at work, attention seeking, like drills into pavements;

walking in a long tunnel of heat, every step a counterweight,
heat like gravity midday. Beyond the tables the sea
continually sparkling, blazing band of distant voices.
I am silent with bubbling water to drink, the shared plate
of bread, my son and daughter conversing. I fell on rocks
yesterday, in a slow cascade like origami unfolding.
Knocking my head. There was a sea of arms to lift me.
I am entering my mother's house like a late invitation.

Afterward I overpay the bill. The waiter runs after me
clutching money. Their honesty is a bouquet I take home

refresh in a vase, the flowers the money did not buy, freely
given. In the sea I am not wounded. I float in a star. My limbs
carried like a mother carries a child too tired to walk.
My walking nearly all done. The walks I cannot walk again.
The sea is a cradle rocking. The sea of my mother's ashes,
the grey dust shrugged out of the jar into the air, fell
into the sea, as we stood together on the promontory,
turning to gold in the water, specks of gold, alchemy.

Atonement

Condemned to sit. My father afraid of not seeing views.
From his armchair in Ealing tests the depth of windows

on walls. Enough to kill you off, the clouds and the cold,
and that was summer. His heart stopped and started

with four shudders. His maxim was *Do as You are Told.*
Three months to live. Unless you pack up for the sun.

An island of donkeys and carts, buzzing bikes like bees
trailing chiffon clouds and everywhere flies. It was hot.

Everyone had a fan and a fly swat. The orange groves
and untouched coast had first sightings of tourists.

On the hill rock upon rock building him as a new man
as if his heart was learning months can be years.

It was a house of redemption. An enforced move
to leave home and to find that beauty is truth & work.

Let's not forget the ampersand. The house of bushes
on the hill of bees was a joy forever like a reprieve.

And the girl who can do nothing right has children
who can do no wrong, a gift of time like forgiveness.

If we could speak, I would say atonement, holding
the page open to insert our presence like restoring

the link in a broken chain, the one beautiful thing
in your name, something to be in our keeping.

Her Place

We've come for what's allowed, to take care of its walls
like a language, like customs we're poorer for losing.
Antonia and *Don Miguel* calling with fresh eggs and a tray

of *coca verda* have a place here; a storm of green water
that ripped away roof tiles and the drive has a place here;
over the dark sea fairy lights on a string of fishing boats

have a place here; the cat *Puig* pronounced Pooch sits here.
My mother has departed with her dog to walk in the woods,
the house waits for her as it waits for us to know our place.

A Note Held

for Bar

A note in a book survives death, the day overcast,
the rain musical, what's dying: separation,
counting the steps in the wood, on the leaf ridden
path, in the next autumn the same isolation
heading into a winter that's fresh, not here yet,
waiting for the daffodils to dawn, the birds elope,
the crow in flight to meet the light on the hill.

Your note embedded in the flyleaf of a book
survives death, time eclipsed or like the pages
closed together, time shut tight, and language
opens time, language unfolds and is moving.
And with handwriting you enter my morning.
What transcends the counting beads of today,
is a fragment of the past like a yellow leaf

caught in the wind brings luck, the talking missed
in isolation and you were always there, I kept
your books shut. The wide door of the future
I enter one day at a time. The trees are turning
into patchwork red and gold, fluorescent in rain.
Memory is held on a thread, fragments become
presence: like words read one at a time in a poem.

Pier in the Rain

All frenzy done. Cinema curtain waves are silken on sand,
closing down, the sea steel grey, the clouds gritty charcoal,
halo mist hovers over distant water, hills loom like mountains,

rain shrouds the coast. With her white brolly tussling with gusts
the Japanese print of her is minimalist, monochrome,
offshore wind at her back, the North Sea suppliant,

every step on the pier is defiant of sense, a joy to the senses,
frame of chiaroscuro with a hint of sepia, all colour drained.
Rain rivets the pier. On close inspection divots are crowns

like pennies thrown from the sky, the pier a running stream.
The colour of January, the colour of Whitby, is a brooch
she pins in her mind, on her old coat, the day after epiphany.

The Table Laid for Grandsons

i

They are sleeping. Storm Dudley is leaving traces,
rattan chairs on their sides again like beached trucks.

Asleep in the guest rooms, empty in the pandemic
ready with clean sheets for the break in the silence
of the house. Last night Dudley was beating fists

ii

on the hillside, whining in Flass Vale while my heart
was racing. We were talking about the war, about Nazis,

self-appointed masters who did not complete their task,
their delusion of a world of underlings had to break
on shores of reality, not on Dunkirk and Moscow

iii

but on Normandy and Stalingrad. Storms ask
for a narrative. Moments of unreality colliding.

It's not yet written. The hoar frost in trust.
My table has guests, the fruit plate covered in grapes
and apples, the physalis nesting in their paper shells.

iv

Harmony in reds and golds, greens and yellows.
My daughter's small painting of roses is propped

by the candle holder. You might miss the eyes of the fox
warning us that life is not all roses, on the dark side
like eyes of storms, juggernauts with crushing wheels.

v

Now I see they are on the same side. Flowers
and predators at risk under our stewardship.

Notes

Guest List in January
Derek Walcott was alive at time of writing in 2015.

About Women
Painting by my daughter Rachel Levitas from a suite about Madame Swann, unreguarded wife in *Remembrance of Things Past* by Proust.

Unbound
145* Ian Bell at Durham v Warwickshire.

The Language of Gesture
We were guests of the Soviet Writers' Union in August 1987.

The Interregnum
The 1987 visit produced *The Poetry of Perestroika* (Iron Press, eds Peter Mortimer and SJ Litherland). Fee of £10 per poem became a fortune at the fall of the rouble in 1991.

Ode to Brummagen
My cousin John Pearce recalled that the terminus was Snow Hill.

Russell Terrace
A two room flat in a large Victorian house.

Errata .
'thou': accuracy to a thousandth of an inch.

Rondo
Jack is Jack Grealish, formerly of Aston Villa.

The Harrowing of the North

England Cricket Board punishment for Durham's £7m upgrading debt (other Test grounds had larger debts.): minus 48 points penalty demoted Durham from Division 1 and enabled Hampshire to stay up. Hampshire's Test ground was included in the eight required for the infamous Hundred. Additional penalties: minus 48 points for 2nd year in Division 2; barred from hosting Test cricket; salaries capped; enforced sale of players. Durham (winners of the County Championship three times in five years) spent 6 years in Division 2. The wrong was righted after 2023 season when Durham topped the group by a huge margin of 66pts for promotion.

Breath of the Virus

refers to Covid needing a host to replicate.

~~The Start of the Season~~

County cricket season cancelled due to first Lockdown.

Upriver

SB Orwell was moored at St Peter's Wharf by 18th century Hammersmith Terrace. Neither the sailing barge nor wharf now exists.

Studentland / Elegy

Durham County Council planning policy favoured conversion of residental homes into student households until City centre streets reached saturation levels. Siegfried Zademack was a Surrealist painter. *Les Jeux Sont Faits*: Croupier call at casino. The chips are down. The die is cast.

A Ghazal for Ian Bell

Ian Bell's last cricket match for Warwickshire 9.9.2020 was away at Glamorgan: scoring 50 and 90. Glamorgan formed a guard of honour.

Allusions
'Allusions rise up to greet me' is a version of an inspiring line from 'The Radiolarians' in Matthew Caley's wonderful surrealist pamphlet *Prophecy is Easy* (Blueprint Press).

In Abandoned Grounds
The former DLI Museum was reprieved when Durham County Council changed hands in 2022. It might not survive any new change.

Inspired by Birds
Second Prize in Concorde competition was a special flight at Mach 2 to the charcoal edge of space above the Bay of Biscay. My son Ben Levitas accompanied me.

Jacqueline
Portrait of Jacqueline Roque (1954).

The Valley of Thorns
'¿Le gusta esta Jardin? ¿Que es suyo? ¡Evite que sus hijos lo destruyan!' is from Malcolm Lowry, *Under the Volcano.*

Thoughts on Mothering Sunday
Troilus and Crysede by Chaucer and *In Memoriam* by Tennyson both feature a house once inhabited by a beloved person now left empty and unlit. The first image seems to have inspired the second.

On Entering *Madroño*
House came back into family ownership after 40 years in October 2022. *Madroño*: name of bush on the site. *Sa Coma de ses Beyes:* hill of bees.

Her Place
Memories/ghosts associated with the house. *Coca verda*: green tart, popular Mallorquin dish.

Acknowledgements

Thanks are due to the editors of the following magazines, anthologies and websites where 39 of these poems first appeared: *The Nightwatchman, Tears in the Fence, Artemis Poetry, New Context: Five, Dreich Magazine Issue I, At the Edge of all Storms, Tabula Rasa, Culture Matters, Bread and Roses Poetry Anthology 2021, Pawnedland, New Boots and Pantisocracies, Bakings, Poetry and Covid, Kitanjali Review.*

My personal thanks for advice and feedback from Annie Wright, Jo Colley, Linda Saunders, Diane Cockburn, Teti Dragas, Cynthia Fuller, Ben Levitas, Rachel Levitas and Vane Women collective.